Self Sabotage

The Definitive Guide to Overcoming Self Sabotage

(The Ultimate Guide to Overcoming Self-sabotaging Behaviour)

Sarah Knowles

Published By **Ryan Princeton**

Sarah Knowles

Self Sabotage: The Definitive Guide to Overcoming Self Sabotage (The Ultimate Guide to Overcoming Self-sabotaging Behaviour)

ISBN   978-1-77485-699-4

No part of this guidebook shall be reproduced in any form without permission in writing from the publisher except in the case of brief quotations embodied in critical articles or reviews.

Legal & Disclaimer

The information contained in this ebook is not designed to replace or take the place of any form of medicine or professional medical advice. The information in this ebook has been provided for educational & entertainment purposes only.

The information contained in this book has been compiled from sources deemed reliable, and it is accurate to the best of the Author's knowledge; however, the Author cannot guarantee its accuracy and validity and cannot be held liable for any errors or omissions. Changes are periodically made to this book. You must consult your doctor or get professional medical advice before using any of the suggested remedies, techniques, or information in this book.

Upon using the information contained in this book, you agree to hold harmless the Author from and against any damages, costs, and expenses, including any legal fees potentially resulting from the application of any of the information provided by this guide. This disclaimer applies to any damages or injury caused by the use and application, whether directly or indirectly, of any advice or information presented, whether for breach of contract, tort, negligence, personal injury, criminal intent, or under any other cause of action.

You agree to accept all risks of using the information presented inside this book. You need to consult a professional medical practitioner in order to ensure you are both able and healthy enough to participate in this program.

Table of Contents

Chapter 1: Staying In A Rut (Lack Of Action)

"Nothing is changed if nothing changes."

I've often heard clients make up fancy speeches to their friends and family members about the things they would like to accomplish, but not always complete. I'm sure that I've stepped on some toes by mentioning this but the reality is that talk isn't cheap. We begin to work on achieving our goals and desires, and we never complete or actually get started.

It's fine to talk about the things you'd like to do in your career, life and business. But without actions you're just being a dreamer and watching life go by. Joel Barker said, "Vision without action is nothing more than an idea. Action without vision is just passing the moment. Vision combined with action could change your globe." What are the things you constantly tell yourself you would like to accomplish but haven't yet achieved? Have you been talking about your goals for a long time and haven't seen any progress? If yes, don't get too hard on yourself as this section is designed intended for you. The first step to success is being honest with yourself in order that you are able to eliminate excuses and continue to move forward. Let's examine Nina's story.

Nina was proactive and you too can take action.

Nina was a teacher for more than 30 years. She was always interested in opening her own school and spoke about it with family members, friends and colleagues. At some time, Nina began her research on the requirements to run and open the school. She looked into grants, government funding and even contacted people she would like to have on her school's board. She not only achieve the first part of her mission however, she also employed an agent in real estate to guide her through various locations where she could begin the school and grow according to the needs over time.

Nina discovered the perfect property at the right location. She made an offer to buy the building and then got it! Nina was so thrilled as her dream was now becoming a reality and everyone who knew about her dream were as thrilled like she.

15 years later, Nina was still waiting to open her school until 15 years later. Nina found herself stuck. Here's how Nina told her story and took action by acquiring

all she required however when it came time to put into place the final plan , she was hesitant. Nina required assistance. Even though it seemed like she was in a good place at early on, it was clear that she was left with no one who could hold her accountable , nor was she taking responsibility to complete her goal. Being stuck in this state led Nina to be overwhelmed and sometimes depressed. After sharing her feelings with a close friend and being encouraged to seek help from an expert who could help her in the right direction and help her to make her dream an actual reality. Nina thought about the suggestions of her friend and, after a couple of days decided to speak with a coach so she could get the college she's always dreamed of.

In working with her coach Nina was able identify different areas of her life in which she was stuck, and she was able to overcome those issues too. Today, Nina's goal is no longer a fantasy and is now an actual fact. With the guidance of her coach, she was able to move in the right direction understanding how to overcome the lack of action and learn how to take consistent actions.

It wasn't because Nina was not proactive and she was not taking consistently actions. There are many times when people start projects in the same way as Nina did, but fail to realize the full potential of it. This kind of behaviour will not just be observed in your professional field however, it can be seen in other areas too. Nina discovered this when she worked with an expert coach. Once you've identified the problem, you must take the appropriate steps to stop this type of self-sabotage. The key step to take in this scenario is to confront the issue head-on. The inaction of others is also a sign of fear. To conquer anxiety, it is important to take it on head-on. For some, it could mean getting an expert to guide you through the steps to confront your fears.

Take the exam on the next page. When you've completed the task, pay careful at other aspects in your life where this type of behavior is evident. It might be necessary to do this exercise again for every area in which this type of behavior is evident in order to take on this type of sabotage.

EXAMINATION EXERCISE

1. Are you able to articulate a plan of your life? If yes, what is it?

2. What steps you've taken to realize your dream a reality?

3. If you've never done anything to start, what is preventing you from beginning?

4. Sometimes, being stuck can manifest throughout our lives. What other areas have your you started something and then not completed?

5. What are the steps you can follow to help you get out of your rut?

6. What are your plans to take any or all of these actions today?

NON-PROGRESSION OF RELATIONSHIPS (NETWORKING)

"The negative of networking is that it doesn't work."

-unknown

No matter if you're looking for work or you are looking to start your own business networking is essential. It is a single area that opens the doors to a variety of possibilities. However, it's the part that requires the most effort. Many find it difficult to make the effort and build a network. This is mostly because of three reasons. These three reasons are all I have observed with numerous clients I've had privilege of dealing with. The primary reason that people are unable to network is because of the difficulty of beginning conversations. I had the privilege of attending a networking training with a friend of mine and she emphasized the necessity of having a plan for networking. She advised the participants to request the names of people who are present at the event. It will help you identify who's there and you will be able to better prepare to engage in conversation and ask the appropriate questions.

Another reason why people struggle with networking is the fear of being rejected. The third reason is the absence of tools for social networking like Meetup and LinkedIn. Some people find it an automatic part of life. This is the place where the introvert-vs. extrovert argument begins.

Networking can be beneficial in a variety of ways. First, it allows you meet like-minded people who are either successful or working towards success. It also helps you make your name known and let people know what you're currently working on or want to accomplish in your professional or business. Thirdly, it's a method to build a following for your company or to get the job you want.

Networking does not only happen at social gatherings and in person, but also online. Numerous websites like LinkedIn, Facebook, & Twitter can be useful ways to meet with people. However certain connections must be established offline. You need to get yourself out there to let others know who you are and also to communicate what you have to offer.

The most important thing to remember about networking is that you only have one chance to make a lasting impression, so you need to do it correctly. If you are handed the opportunity to present your business at an event, and follow up after a few days, keep in mind that it is your chance to promote your company or yourself since you are only given one chance. If the person at the other end of the line doesn't feel that you are appealing and appealing, then you will not be able to create a second impression.

Discover the key of networking by Steve

Steve is currently working in a job that she is not enjoying. She was constantly looking to find a job with another company, interviewing whenever she could but was not having any success with the hunt. A few days ago, while browsing on an online social network, Steve came across a networking event specifically for professionals. Steve has never been scared to meet new individuals however this was the first time she had attended an event for networking, so she was a bit nervous. She decided to go ahead and signed up for the event, hoping of getting to know new people.

A couple of days later, Steve attended the networking event. Steve was stunned by the amount of professionals in attendance, which created an increase in anxiety. Steve offered herself a motivational speech and then began to mingle and mix with other professionals present. The more she interacted with the other professionals, the less anxiety she felt.

Steve has collected the name and contact information of people who she spoke to. As she was doing this she was able to meet with a business owner looking to employ someone with her expertise. Steve and the owner of the business agreed to meet with one other in a couple of days during lunch. The next day, Steve landed the job. If she hadn't taken the time to build relationships, she could be stuck for a bit longer in a position she was not enjoying.

In the previous chapter, I discussed introverts as opposed to. extroverts in relation to networking. Extroverts feel a sense of satisfaction by meeting new people and engaging in social networking. Introverts gain energy by being in a room, getting energized by going back to try to do it again. Some suggestions for introverts with regards to networking include: First, ask someone to introduce yourself if you are afraid of speaking to strangers. This could help alleviate some of your anxieties to allow you to have an engaging conversation. In the second instance, if you are unable to introduce yourself with the help of a person else is a problem attempt to initiate an exchange in a different manner. For example, instead of engaging in conversation using the traditional method of asking, "Hello. What's up?" You can change the tone of conversation by using the phrase,

"Tell me more about your work or profession or maybe the beautiful watch you're sporting." This can help make a connection and start conversations that are less stressful.

The key to growth in your business or career is networking. Set yourself the goal of attending at least two networking events per month. This will allow you to develop the habit of stepping outside your comfort zone, and set your journey towards success.

EXAMINATION EXERCISE

1. On a scale from 0 to 10 How do you fare in networking?

2. What are the biggest challenges you have to overcome in terms of networking?

3. After having read about Steve What is the best method to get over your challenges with networking?

4. Search for networking events happening in your region. Make sure you look for networking events that align with your goals. For instance, you shouldn't go to a gathering that is geared towards book lovers if are trying to establish your retailer of clothing. Set a goal at the time you go to any networking event. I recommend attending at least two networking events a month. It doesn't matter if it's to get an employment opportunity or to gain customers for your business. Make a plan and make sure to follow up within a couple of days.

Chapter 2: Little Wins!

Celebrate Small wins

Who wouldn't like to succeed in life? Your success is based on achieving goals. These goals can add value for your existence and provide you an identity. Have you ever tried to achieve a goal but then give up on the route? Did you ever begin working towards a goal, but later realize it was too complex and gave the project up? Have you ever had the feeling that you're making the effort required, you it doesn't seem to get you anyplace?

If you've ever felt like this, then you're not all alone. I've had times when I was in the same boat. The issue is that we are all a bit too harsh on ourselves and then quickly penalize ourselves. We judge poor performance quickly. We've all been taught to believe that failure is a bad thing. This mindset is always in your way and hinder you from reaching your goals. I've seen this in my personal experiences. Therefore, I began to think about what the secret behind achieving this goal was? I've often thought, what's the main different between those who have succeeded and those who don't? After some research I realized it's all about the mindset and perspective. In this article you'll learn about something we should be doing: celebrate the small victories that happen in our lives. If you're quick to scold yourself for your mistakes that you've made, you should be equally fast to celebrate your successes as well.

Your point of view

Most people tend to believe that success is due to the luck of their hands or natural talents. True, luck plays some part, as does the ability. However, there's more to the success equation than these two components. Your attitude towards life and all that goes with it are important. I'm sure you've heard something about Thomas Edison. In fact, he did create the bulb that lights up. Did you realize it would take Edison over 10,000 attempts to design the lightbulb? Edison certainly fought through all obstacles and achieved success. He was not deterred each time he failed and instead used his failures to propel him towards success.

Why not take a leaf from Edison's story and emulate his success? It's fine to make mistakes, but it's not acceptable to abandon the cause. It's all about your attitude and your outlook. Do not try to be an idealist. It's fine to try to be perfect but it's not okay to quit when you fail. It's all about attempting to make improvements to your self. It's quite easy to take your punishments when you fail; but what happens to the accomplishments you achieve? I would suggest changing your attitude towards failing. It's fine to feel guilty about failing however it's not ok to discredit any success you make.

Small wins are important.

If you're looking to reach success, be aware that it isn't going to be achieved over night. It could take one week or even a whole year. Be prepared and concentrate on your goals. It's okay to consider the larger perspective. But, when you are on this process, you should not neglect the little steps that you have to complete to achieve your ultimate target. You must not only acknowledge the small victories and celebrate them, but also acknowledge your successes. We tend to lose motivation. You need drive to continue If you continue decreasing it, you'll not be able to achieve your

objectives. Motivational issues usually arise from uncertainty regarding how far your goals

go. Sometimes, we are prone to think that the targets are quite far off and we fail to notice things right beneath our feet. If you search for it, you'll see that success is just in front of

you. Every little goal you accomplish will provide you with the determination and motivation to continue to push forward regardless of challenges and obstacles.

Learn to appreciate

Through my experience I discovered that appreciation is a must -- a virtue that we often overlook. We tend to forget to appreciate everything we've done and accomplished and are instead focused on what we've failed to achieve. Be grateful and acknowledge every step you take , and each small victory you win. This could be what the difference between success and failing. You should give yourself a pat on the back each time you accomplish something. Remember, you are the only one to have achieved an objective. Be proud of the little things and you'll feel more confident about your accomplishments.

Successful habits

In the previous chapter you learned about the different ways you can begin incorporating changes into your lifestyle. Utilize these tips to create your own successful routine. The path to success isn't easy without an established routine. It isn't feasible to have a routine without creating habitual habits. It may not be simple to develop effective habits, but you can make the process easier for yourself by celebrating small successes. Rememberthat you're getting ready for a race. You must develop an incentive system that will ensure that your brain becomes used to a desire for the achievement.

This moment

You can't alter the past and you can't anticipate the future. One thing you are able to influence is your present. Your attitude towards the present will define your future. Do not take the present as a given. It may not be important to you now However, what you do now will affect the future of your life. Put your money into yourself and your goals. Making small investments over a long time is the only way to achieve success. Although they may seem small today, a blend of these events in time will lead to the success you desire. Let's say, for instance, imagine that you would like to learn how to play the guitar. A few hours today, and learning the chords on a guitar isn't an important thing. But if you stay practicing often, eventually you'll be able to master the art of learning you can play guitar.

The steps to success

Five simple steps that you can follow to achieve success. Use these steps to win small victories too. If you are able to win something is a great incentive to continue.

First, you must create some goals that are big for you. After you have set your major goals, it is important to reduce them to smaller goals. If you accomplish a small goal, be sure to reward yourself. You can pat yourself in the back to acknowledge a task you've done well. Only you is able to achieve your goals. There is no one else who will be able to do it for you. Therefore, you must be able to celebrate every triumph that you encounter regardless of how large or small.

Set up a reward system for yourself. It doesn't need to be anything extravagant. It's as easy as giving yourself a day in the spa or buying the bag you've always wanted is an incentive in itself. It's good to set goals because they provide you with a reason to live your life. However, you shouldn't allow your goals to overwhelm you. This will only increase the chances of becoming overwhelmed and giving up completely.

Start tracking the progress you've made. As you begin to see your progress even if it's just taking one small step at a moment this is still a significant step and improves confidence in yourself. One aspect is crucial of your life that is something you have to alter if wish to achieve success and overcome negative thought. You need to work on changing your outlook. Sometimes, it can be hard to focus on your goals while forgetting about the rest of your life. Make sure you don't lose your focus on your daily life when trying to achieve your objectives. Adjust your mindset and take positive attitudes towards your life. Every obstacle you encounter is simply a bump in your path, and it doesn't mean it's the end. It's only at an end when you quit and tell yourself that.

Appreciate Your Life

I am always amazed of people who succeeded in changing their lives in radical ways. People who travel around the world and seem to be in complete peace. They have been able to clear their homes and live on the contents of a backpack. People who raise funds for charity or participate in marathons. People who change their job or relocate halfway across the globe or start their own business. When I see all the people who are striving to achieve their goals and changing their lives, I am awestruck. Before, I would struggle with any major, life-altering change. If I saw the people I admired I felt jealous of their success.

As I worked on reframing my mental outlook, It became clear that there wasn't any jealousy I felt. My feeling was one of discontent. Sometimes when you've had a tiring day, photos of an Instagram traveler might make you feel just a little small amount of at times. It is possible that you don't desire the sort of lifestyle that the traveler has and your envy could be due to the fact that they take on the challenges more easily than youdo, they are able to deal with uncertainty and make changes with more confidence than you. You might not want to race a marathon, or even explore across the globe. It's possible that you are still noticing the green-eyed monster scurrying around at times.

If the situation occurs, it implies that you have to alter your perception of your life. You should begin to appreciate your life. It's possible that you haven't done similar things to what others havedone, however that doesn't mean that you've not done something. You may have made a few important decisions in your life that you didn't even realize that you had done it. Do not try to minimize your little wins since they aren't as important like the accomplishments that other people have accomplished. Every person has a story behind them and so do you. It's not necessary to be down about the actions of other people are doing. There are achievements you can take pride in. The earlier you recognize this the more satisfied you'll be. If you're unhappy with the job you're currently working in and you're looking for another job. If you're unhappy about the way you live your life, you should make few adjustments. If you are constantly unhappy with your life, determine reasons for why you feel this way and put in the effort to build the kind of life you're content with. You can make a change in your life however only when you're ready to. Instead of looking at other people and feeling down about yourself, why not make steps in a positive direction?

Why not spend some time doing things you love? Spend time with those you are passionate about. Spend more time working on your personal growth. Invest in yourself. Do not seek happiness from external sources. Your happiness is on your shoulders. It is important to be aware of this sooner than later.

When you experience the slightest hint of jealousy or envy take the time to step back and adjust your perception. It is important to accept that your life will alter and is currently changing. You're not the person you were. There was a time when you wanted certain things as young, but those requirements changed once you were an adult, and they changed when you became an adult. As an example, when you were a young person perhaps you wanted to be your own person. As an adult and you are in this situation, you may desire something different. In this course of action you should not forget that you have achieved the goal you set for yourself in your youth.

Don't try to compare your experience with another's. Everyone goes through their own adventures and follow different paths through life, therefore trying to expect the same outcomes isn't wise. If you ever feel bewildered, think about the cause of your feeling of jealousy, particularly if you do not want to reach the same goals that other people are achieving.

Find ways to celebrate your life and be happy about your little wins. It can be like keeping your home clean. Be aware of your language choices with yourself. Make sure you maintain a positive outlook toward life and yourself. If, for instance, you've completed every task on your list this is a tiny success. Why shouldn't you celebrate this? It is important to celebrate every success that you can get. In the event that you don't, who else? In the event that you've paid down a credit card or credit card debt you're a winner too. You deserve a high-five for getting to this point. It's not an easy road and yet you've succeeded in getting to this point. As I've said, everybody has a story to tell. Don't take the tiniest part of someone else's story and base your own life on it. It's not fair to yourself or anyone else in your life.

Take a step towards the right direction and begin taking note of yourself.

How small wins can be effective

Everyone is waiting for the breakthrough that will be the moment that is magical or similar to this, that will make everything click. Most of us instinctively or unconsciously expend hours trying to locate this important breakthrough. We look for that moment that everything is in placeperhaps when you earn promoted or win a contest, or sing the song flawlessly. These are all definitely rewarding, and it's appropriate to seek them out. But there is an issue with this type of thinking. If you focus on the ultimate goal in your life, you're actually overextending yourself. If you aren't able to achieve this goal due to the fact that it's not feasible, you set yourself up for failure. Breakthroughs aren't often seen. They are not common, hence the name. When you're looking for that major break you don't look for every other tiny steps that will assist you in reaching your desired goal. You overlook the small aspects of life. You don't think about the little steps you can take and the tiny wins that are awaiting you.

People who have achieved success in their lives aren't involved in the quest to find the perfect opportunity. Instead, they choose to take an action that is messy and impactful, and look for smaller breakthroughs. Even small victories which may seem minor at first, it will be worth it over time. Every tiny step you take and every win that you achieve will get you one step closer to achieving your grand target. If you don't remember this, you're making yourself vulnerable to disappointment. It is best to enjoy an ongoing stream of small successes rather than putting your time and effort trying to find an elusive breakthrough. Little steps will definitely aid you in achieving your goals in your life.

If you're looking to achieve your goal, you require discipline and determination. But, perseverance and tenacity are vital to your success as well. One of the most significant problems you'll encounter in your life is the absence of a proper plan. When you try to get quick results, you let your insanity get over you. In the end, impatience can lead to frustration and will squelch any motivation that you might have. In some cases people are scared to take the first step due to their fears of the unknown. Instead of allowing the anxiety to hold you back make a move. It doesn't need to be an important thing or even a tiny step can be enough. Start small, and take a moment to be proud of your accomplishments and you'll feel more confident about yourself. After several weeks, you'll be able to see some improvement to your mood. All the negativity you felt about certain tasks or actions will fade when you take that first step. You've won half the fight the moment you make the first step.

The Progress Principle

Teresa Amabile and Stephen Kramer collaborated for a long time in the development of the The Progress Principle. It was developed by Stephen Kramer and Teresa Amabile. Principle was developed primarily to help understand the many aspects that helped inspire and motivate employees to be their best while making them feel happy. I came to realize that the concepts that are outlined by the Principle can be applied to every aspect of our lives. Utilizing the ideas discussed in this article it is possible to improve your efficiency while keeping your positive attitude toward the world.

Progress is steady

Small losses can affect your psychological state. Thus, be happy with the small victories and you will experience an impact on your life. It is more beneficial to work steadily rather than pursuing an impossible breakthrough. Amabile and Kramer recognized that a positive attitude towards their inner work was vital to make progress. When you achieve progress, it will fill you with positive emotions such as self-confidence and happiness, which in turn boosts your self-esteem. This is in turn, increases the efficiency of your work. If you're brimming with positive feelings this provides you with an increase in energy and willpower, which boosts the overall performance. If you feel confident about your own work, it improves and so does your productivity.

Creativity and motivation

If you are able to accomplish something and make a habit of continuous growth and your motivation levels increase. This can, in turn, boost your enthusiasm for your work and your personal life. People who are driven by their inner drive will perform better in all aspects of life. Motivation and creativity often work together. If you're driven and creative, your level of thinking are elevated. If you've got an inner desire to achieve something and possess the required drive and discipline to go through with it, you'll find creative ways to reach your objectives. If you enjoy your work and you are able to come up with better ways to complete your job. This principle is applicable to any aspect of your life.

Catalysts, nourishers and catalysts.

Certain things can encourage progress such as clear objectives and resources, adequate time, help needed and autonomy. If all these elements are present, your potential to achieve success is increased. Certain aspects can help you advance in your life. Your circle of friends, your how you handle your difficulties, and your attitude are all essential to your advancement. If you are in a negative work atmosphere, your performance will decline. However when you're around people who are filled with positive energy and working in a positive working environment, your efficiency will grow. It is essential to be aware of the various things that can act as catalysts and also sources of growth within your own life. Once you have identified the issues then you can begin working on them.

Progress journal

It is essential to track your progress. If you realize you've walked an amount of distance and keep written down the progress acknowledging your accomplishments becomes simpler. Start maintaining your progress journal. Record all the things you complete in a given day in your journal. Also, create an outline of the goals you'd like to accomplish. In addition, make an eye on the various methods you'd like to use to make improvements to yourself. If the same situation was to arise in the near future What would you do to it? How do you respond to this? This question can help to give you a sense control over the reactions you take.

Chapter 3: The Turning Point Of Procrastination

There's no doubt there are times when we may be so entangled in procrastination that no piece advice can get us out of it. So, what do you do if this is the situation? Are you willing to allow your life to be destroyed? It's a given that things will not be this way! In films, it's common for stories to choose the "nuclear alternative" when everything else has failed. This is particularly applicable to the issue of beating the deep-rooted habit of procrastination.

For life coaches and psychologists there is a method known as "structured procrastination". In a way, taking the technical meaning of these terms that is, simply, that you can turn procrastination into productive. In this section, you'll be required to sift through your the previous knowledge of fancy tricks and strategies to turn procrastination into something more productive. We don't claim that the method mentioned above is the most effective, but it is a fact that has been proven it: it actually works.

How does this approach perform? The famous to-do-list is required to be used here. You can now add your task to the "most crucial" thing on the list. It's the task you've been waiting for and have put off. Look over the list you currently have, and then add those chores or tasks you must complete during the day. They can be organized in accordance with urgency or any other criteria you prefer. In the past the list ought to be getting in length and become more thorough. Things such as "washing dishes" or "downloading the most recent NCIS episode" NCIS" ought to have been added to the list.

Next, you must classify the items in such a way that items with deadlines that are more flexible are placed into"priority. "priority" section. This is sure to place the project you've put off to in the bottom of your list. Note that because this task that was once a priority was pushed down to the bottom of the list, it's more appealing for your unconscious mind to focus on it.

Do your dishes in the sink. While you're doing this, review of the checklist again. It's tempting to put off in washing the dishes, then move on to what's the "important task" that's been pushed down the list. Procrastination is used to its advantage!

John Perry, emeritus professor of philosophy at Stanford University, reminded people that the efficacy of this method is based on their capacity to deceive themselves. If you consider itthis way, you're manipulating yourself to work towards those things that have been distorted priorities. This is not a problem. Many studies have proven that people who routinely delay their work do not have the best skills at deceiving themselves. Their minds are at work when they mix between the concepts of long and short-term goals.

Are there other aspects than this method? Yes, there is! Do you remember the feeling of anxiety that is associated with your lack of ability to finish your the tasks? Check it out and see how it has changed into motivation as you go through the process of systematically avoiding procrastination! When you observe the items on your list getting completed each day, that is the moment you be able to see that you've turned procrastination into productive. There are numerous tips other resources can offer in

the fight against
procrastination. There is the
certainty that this one is the most
simple and efficient!

Chapter 4: Self-Improvement Work A 30-Day Challenge To Become The Best Version Of Yourself

For the start of the segment I'd like you to be aware that positive thoughts can alter your brain. Keep in mind all the memes you encounter in Facebook, Twitter, Instagram, Tumblr, etc. It is possible that they can make you angry sometimes because the flow of information is so fast however, holding the anger in is like having a drink of poison, and hoping for another person to be dead. The more that an individual's thought patterns trend negative and slip into rumination--continually turning over a situation in one's mind and focusing on its negative aspects-- the easier it becomes to return automatically to these thought patterns. The effects of ruminating could cause damage to brain structures which control emotions as well as memory and emotions. The shackles that many of us are encased can be extremely unhealthy. That being said it is time to break the old self that we've created and the person we've taught us to believe we are, to learn to train our brains to concentrate on happiness, joy and gratitude. You can let go of the things that aren't you and become what you believe you're and what you're here to accomplish. When you're in any current situation in which there is a chance to become self-aware and aware, I would like you to take a deep dive into the question, "What would someone who truly loves themselves take on?" When I say love, I am referring to something you probably aren't familiar with , if you really looked back on your entire life. Sigmund Freud described libido as "the emotion, thought of as a numerical amount ... from the feelings that are associated with everything contained in the word "love"." It is not libido. What I'm referring to is love that is unconditional and gratitude. What does someone who truly is grateful for themselves do? It's so easy however, it is becoming more complicated. You will discover that simplicity implies complication and merely means complication in real life.

What I see most often is that people are stuck in their lives, as we all have an experience that we can't be free of. This can be a huge obstacle to performance and specific areas of our success and our lives. This is due to the fact that we all have a an impression of "trauma," which triggers painful memories either false or true. It drains us of vitality, and we believe "This could occur again." "After everything,, history repeats itself, doesn't it?" So, we look forward to and fear situations that we don't like and refuse to relax. We might think that to ourselves "I am not sure I could let this go or let it go" But to me it is possible that, there is a way to let go. It's not just about your past, or even the reader's history sitting right next to you. I don't care about how bad your past was, and I'm talking about grave histories. It could be the sex of a child, or a death within the family, or any other grievances or perhaps you were victimized as a child or a vehicle accident that you've had to endure, or you've been through long periods of hospitalization as a result of persistent health issues. You can get rid of. It is possible to do it. It is important to let go of the past since right now, you believe that If it isn't allowed to let the thoughts of your past disappear in some way, your future is opened to negative events or events that you would rather not have. The memories are stored in our minds are simply hang-ups and that's the thing you need to be reminded of. The past that is reoccurring in our minds are simply hang-ups, yet we believe that it's real and real and so vivid. What we are robbed of from our lives, which is the mind of our own. The past is just a notion. It's not true. The future isn't true either, as it is an interpretation on the previous. We perceive things as we see them, not in the way that the thing is, and that also includes the past. That conversation, which you believed was a heated debate over telephone with the person who was on the line was not really an argument. What you believe you know about people are actually just a ruse. You have no knowledge of their lives, regardless of what they might lead you to believe. Consider a painful moment in your life you'd like to get rid of. Once you've thought about it, imagine experiencing the incident and all the emotions and feelings associated with the event. It's a guided imagination exercise designed to help with let go about the events of your past.

Do this while keeping your eyes shut however, since you're doing this, you can perform this "closed-eyed" variation of the exercise yourself. I would like you to be relaxed and be aware of your breathing. Breathe with your mouth at your usual pace, but pay attention to the breath. And then exhale through your mouth at your usual pace. Keep doing this. After that, I'd like you to (while being aware the sound of your breath) pay attention to your body and the sensations you feel within your body. Consider how your buttocks feel sitting on a stool or someplace else. Continue to focus on the sensation. When you've realized that you're conscious the body you are in, I'd like you to imagine this thought "You don't have a any future." "The the future will be completely unknowable." "You have been completely present in this moment. Everything else is irrelevant." Then I'd like you to believe that the past has never occurred. The past is just a myth, and you've always been exactly where you are now right now, here. What you feel inside your body, your perceptions you're experiencing or even the vision that you experience through your closed eyes. It's all real. It's happening right in the present. Consider that. You don't have to dwell on it. Simply be present. It is possible to be skeptical and think, "Well, I understand that the past doesn't exist in the same way that where I am today is but it still influences me." I'm sure, you might have to dig into your soul to find a way to overcome your past. there are likely other ways that you have to seek out. There is no Morpheus in "The Matrix" with the blue pill that can close the chapter so that you will be able to get back in the morning and belie in whatever you wish to be convinced of. It is important to be aware that the primary reason for recalling these events in your head, repeatedly and over and over again, is that you allow your mind to drift away from the present moment, which is where you are at the moment.

I would like you to repeat this phrase in my absence. "I believe that, and therefore, I am. I can see that I am aware, so am I conscious?" Here's the far-fetched scope of this initial idea. What is an idea? What is awareness? Take a moment to listen. We consider our thoughts through the lens of words, symbols, calculations and images. A lot of our opinions, thoughts, and perceptions connect us to reality. What happens when the shattered web of beliefs fall in front of you?

What happens is that you'll program your mind to doubt all you believe to have learned about reality. You'll allow your feelings to be a part of and accept reality for what it is. This is a part of everything that science and religion God and money, social systems and your body, brain as well as your socialization, education as well as your life's mission society, economy and business, people, relationships and the entire universe. Whatever you want to call it and it's likely to be challenged. Be aware of the realities. It is likely that you are writing in your head ideas and concepts of reality. The most eye-opening thing is the fact that reality exists independent of thought. Anybody's thought.

Are you aware? We all think that we are conscious. The mind is aware of concepts of labels, images and labels, or the emotions that result from the mental state. If I were to grab an eraser and to draw the illustration of an electrical socket, and there was a blank wall, it would be facing your drawing. It happens somehow, the drawing was to show a photo of a face. Or maybe it's an emoticon that you can find on the internet in some way, by accident. What brought the image to light?

You could first think it's just the top portion of the wall socket because that's the original drawing, and nothing more, less less.Or you could say, "No. It's the face. It's clear it is there right on the central part of the image." You can also claim, "It is both the face as well as the socket. that socket." It is possible to be a little condescending , but clever and say "It really is art. It's not."

If we're going to break any type of code of awareness and progress to different levels of consciousness, we have to be able to see, irrespective of our thoughts projecting onto the image, that what it is, in all its entirety, is ink blots on the page.

My aim to you the readers is to convey my thoughts with sensitivity to the best of my ability. I will provide you with the guideline, a thirty day map of the territory that I will provide to you to enable you to become the best version of you. I can't force authentic behaviour from you, for example, raising your awareness levels or self-awareness. You can try to practice the fundamental self-awareness process by constantly reminding yourself that "I have eaten, breathing I am speaking and I am resting etc." throughout the course of your life. All is yours to decide. There's no guarantee that I can change your mind or encourage you to act psychologically through raising your awareness, the mind, or imaginings such as the enlightenment.

Before I begin my educational content of this text, I need to determine the direction this book is going to follow. I've mentioned earlier, Abraham Maslow, and his term 'Self-Actualization'. It was inspired by Maslow's well-known "Hierarchy of Needs" that is widely taught in a variety of Psychology 101 courses. The 5 levels of the Hierarchy of Needs include Physical and Psychological Needs (Basic Needs) Safety Needs, Affection and Love Needs Esteem Needs (which must be regularly reviewed) as well as Self-Actualization needs. This Occam's Razor method is my for every chapter in this book. We'll start at the beginning, moving to intermediate and finally, we'll try to reach the level of mastery or advanced.

Chapter 5: What To Do Thwart Others' Attempts To Defeat You

The world will attempt to beat your efforts. It's not just you. person with a winning attitude. There are many other winners in the world, competing for the top spot. They are skilled and ruthless in winning. However, you have to beat them to stay in the lead. So, you have to figure ways to stop the ones who want to overtake you. You need to find an approach to beat them and win regardless of cost.

The act of sabotage requires a certain amount of moral immorality. It is, after all, not the most pleasant thing to do. It is important to put aside the side of you that wants to please others and wants to win more than being a good friend or pleasing others. Keep in mind that being nice does mean you will be

successful in your life. Nobody will
be able to reciprocate the kindness
you show to them. They'll simply
jump on your back and take what
you desired. Don't try to be nice,
and instead be brutal. Get rid of
the notion that you're doing
something wrong by trying to
undermine your
adversaries. Perhaps it's immoral
however morals are merely false
concepts that have been created
by society to enable the powerful
to advance over those less
powerful.

Also, you should let go of the
persistent anxiety that you're not
enough to beat your adversaries. It
is possible. However terrifying or
intimidating your adversary is, you
are able to beat him to dust. You're
in the right position but you must
adopt a winning mindset and trust
that you can beat yourself with
your entire heart. It's time to stop
believing that you're not as good
as others, or that other people are

going to beat you. Your confidence can help you beat the competition. Therefore, be positive and trust in your abilities with all your heart.

It's helpful to meet others who are also believers and who are willing to encourage and praise you. If you have a group who are cheering for you You won't be able to let them down and you'll trust in your abilities. This boosts your motivation and confidence to beat your adversaries. But, if you're all by yourself in this battle it's fine. You can create a fan-base as you win more and show people that they can trust your abilities. Use that as a reason to drive you to succeed. Don't let the feeling of loneliness or insecurity cause you to feel down or convince you that you're not worthy of winning simply because nobody else is as confident in you.

It is time to stop being a victim and stop thinking about yourself as an underdog, too. Although there are many touching films about the underdogs who rise to the top however, they are not based on actual events. In reality it's sharks with bloodlust, brutality and bloodlust who always come out at the top. Think of yourself as the shark in this story and you will win.

Block Other's Snarkiness

It is essential not to allow people to intimidate you. They'll certainly attempt to intimidate you. Intimidation is a winning strategy that I'll teach you to master later. There are many others who are going to try it, and may succeed. However, you can stop the attempts of others to intimidate by acknowledging the truth of it and not allowing yourself to be influenced by the idea. One person may smirk or appear to be the most prestigious of them all but it's only an act of deceit. It's not necessary to doubt it.

Don't be fooled by people try to bluff. Some will attempt to convince you to stop before you begin with a spiel about how large and weak they are. They'll say they have all the resources required to win, and they will claim that they have more friends, more resources and even more abilities to help them win. However, remember that they can only succeed if you let them. You can keep them from your tricks, by not allowing yourself to be a victim of their lies. Know that life is similar to poker. People generally have great poker faces and can make you believe their deceit. They're most likely lying.

If someone tries to convince that you let them prevail, or make you feel like letting them win, you have to be aware of what they are doing. They don't deserve your love or sympathy. Don't be fooled by their tricks. They're trying to trick you. This is a effective winning tactic that we discuss in Chapter 3. It is possible to pretend that you feel regretting them or admire them and let them win in order for them to relax and let their guards fall. But remain as brutal as you have been in real life.

When someone is trying to take advantage of you Don't allow them to. You're ahead of the curve because you'll be aware of all the tricks that are in the book when you're done reading this. If someone attempts to use a winning strategy against you, you'll are aware of what he is up to and how you are able to block it. Simply refuse to believe the idea. You can pretend you have, for the sake of a entertainment however you don't have to. People will take any action to beat you, so prepare.

Be the last one to throw Stones

If you're the first person to join fight it is often the first one to exhaust of energy. It is better to arrive early, but prepared. When you have made your mind to pursue something in your life Don't tell anyone about it. Begin planning, preparing and getting yourself prepared. Create a strategy to achieve what you would like. Find allies to support you. Get information about your adversaries. Develop your skills and, while doing so do not reveal to anyone what you're going after.

When the time is right that no one else is waiting take action and place your name into the hat to win what you would like to win. Your opponents are exhausted fighting for victory and you can leverage that for your benefit. In addition, the opponents aren't prepared to face you as a potential adversary, and therefore they do not have strategies to fight you. This is a fantastic strategy taught by Sun Tzu in his The Art of War. It's really effective. Be careful not to get lazy or spend too much time. Don't fall for an illusion of security due to the fact that you're slow to play. Your adversaries could very quickly come up with strategies to defeat you, so stay alert and prepared immediately.

Use anything as a weapon

When you are fighting someone in a particular area, you could quickly transform any object into a weapon that you can defeat him. While we will discuss the subject in greater detail In Chapter 5 we'll discuss some of the most basic aspects here.

You can make use of your adversaries weaknesses to make him feel weaker. You can tell him that he's not sufficient or convince him that he's not worth it. If he is self-defeating and self-esteem, it can cause him to fall. It is possible to identify his weaknesses through his interactions with others. Make use of them to your best ability.

It is also possible to take on his family members. The breaking up of his relationships or causing strife within his family can cause him to lose motivation and take off his strength.

If he is dependent on anything, for example, his connections or physical power, attack that item and eliminate it. Turn his connections against him. Restrict his access or shut off all access to the tools could help him advance. Make him appear unprofessional or weak to make others doubt in his abilities. You could seriously harm your chances by removing the tools he has and his friends.

If you are aware of something sinister about your adversary You can leverage that against him. You can either blackmail him or spread the information anonymously all over the world to discredit him. This is a great method to block competitors from an opening or new job within a business such as. Make use of tools such as social media and the state's criminal arrest records to uncover the truth about his past including unprofessional posts or photos that are dirty and extra marital relationships, accusations of abuse and private political views as well as criminal histories from the past or any other information that could make him look bad. Make sure to expose the information as you think it is necessary to cause people to turn against him. This is a common tactic used in politics, in which one candidate utilizes the past history of his voting as well as criminal records to defame opponents.

It is possible to use the biases of those around you to benefit. If you're competing with an individual for a position of leadership at work. You each work for an progressive organization that promotes liberal values , but is averse to more conservative beliefs. It is obvious that you can influence the majority of employees within the organization to be against the other candidate if you disclose that he voted for republicans during the last election. Examine the field to evaluate individuals for their beliefs and values. Use that information to gain supporters and to smear your opponents. The more support you receive in return, and also the support you get out of your opponents the greater chance you have to succeed in what you've worked for.

It could also work effective if you're trying to get a date with one another. Find out what the person believes and what you believe in. And then, you can tell each of them they are incompatible due to their different the way they vote or their lifestyle. This could stop their love affair before it begins and boost your chances of securing the chance to have a date.

Learn the plans of your adversaries. If he's planning an event for a press conference on a particular day, you should have a better plan the day prior. If he's trying to convince certain people to join the cause, try to offer them better deals. If he has plans to go on an evening with someone you like, work out how to secure an appointment in advance or appear at the same restaurant to sabotage the date. Make use of his battle plans to come up with your own strategy to defeat him. Stop every move he makes before he even thinks about it. It's all about being aware of when he is likely to do.

Take All That You Can Stride

Your adversary has discovered
ways to harm you. He's either said
something demeaning to
undermine your self-esteem or
handed you a serious blow. What's
the best method to deter his efforts
to take you down? Let this blow
slide off your shoulders. Keep
smiling and keep plugging on.

When you don't admit defeat or
display your pain You accomplish
a lot of things. First, you make
your opponent feel
intimidated. He'll be amazed at
how you're not easily injured or
shaken. You also show your
strength and demonstrate that you
are able to move forward with the
fight regardless of what it is
regardless of how much your
adversaries try to knock you
over. You also gain the respect of
your fellows when they see you
rise up , wash your clothes, and
get to work. People appreciate

those who aren't willing to be impeded by the opposition. You'll earn brownie points.

Do not dwell on the shame or the pain that your opponent did to you, concentrate on problem-solving. Find ways to reduce the issue. Discover ways to continue to move forward. It's crucial to take a deep breath, then take inventory of the damage done

Chapter 6: Limitation Caused By Self-Sabotage And How To Get Over Them

You could think about these questions whenever you find yourself stuck in patterns that cause problems in your life and prevent you from reaching your goals. While you attempt to modify and disrupt these patterns, in a way, you are at the same place every time. If you find yourself in a pattern that is adolescent and you are able to undermine the self-sabotage you have created. Self-sabotage refers to actions or patterns that hinder you and stop your from carrying out what want to accomplish.

What is it like?

You may be able to threaten your own with a variety of methods. Certain are obvious. However, some aren't as easy to spot.

Slamming other people when things go wrong

Most of the time, bad things happen and are not the fault of anyone else. It's possible that bad luck may be the fault of another person, but this isn't always the case.

If you are prone to finding problems in other areas whenever you encounter problems, it might be worthwhile taking a more thorough look at the part you had in the incident. If your partner has relationship issues that affect you each other. You decide they are not going to change and you also decide to split with them. You are elated about the breakupbecause the fact that they were hesitant to change stopped you from continuing to live together. Your friends agree that you made the right choice. But, if, however, you don't spend some time to understand the ways you might have contributed to the problems because of the relationship, according to Maury Joseph PsyD and you squander your chance to discover and gain from the learning.

Choosing to leave when the situation is not working

There's nothing wrong with moving away from situations that don't match your expectations. This could be among the most efficient options. It's advisable to make a quick exit and check to see whether you've made an effort. It is possible that you are not able to be able to stay at work for a long time. You left one job because of the fact that your manager abused you. You were dismissed for a second time because of the fact that you were overstaffed. Your next job was terminated because of toxic colleagues, and many other. These are legitimate reasons but a typical pattern could have much

deeper. Unpredictability about your ability to perform well or maintain a steady pace can lead to errors that affect your productivity or stop you from thriving in the

workplace. Perhaps you're scared of resentment or disapproval. It's difficult to overcome, but removing obstacles and problems helps you expand your. If you let go prior to putting with a lot of effort and effort, you might not know how to change your options to the next time.

Laziness

Have you been a bit sluggish or stuck when you had to complete a crucial task? It's not uncommon to experience this.

You've prepared, completed all your research, set your feet to begin and then realize that you could not get started. Your enthusiasm has completely gone away. You can now relax from your task by clearing out the fridge, organizing your junk room or launching an action-movie marathon.

Negligence may occur without apparent reason, but it usually has anunderlying motive, like:

You are confused about the in the time frame being doubtful of your abilities or ability, fighting with partners or friends

You are able to slowly deteriorate yourself (along with causing harm to your relationships) in a variety of ways.

It's always a good idea to make suggestions to others, even when it's about things that aren't important for example, such as the restaurant you last attended. You can also indicate prompt responses, like leaving an unclean cooking area or "overlook" crucial dates.

However you may get angry fast or even take things personal regardless of whether they're directed towards you or not. Maybe you're having difficulty talking with your partner about what you feel, particularly when you're in a state of distress. Therefore, you resort to snark, and more casual hostility in contrast to more effective methods of interaction.

You're dating people who aren't for you

Self-sabotaging actions are usually seen within partnerships. People who don't complete all the boxes is one of the most common types of self-sabotage.

You may:

Continue to be in contact with a similar type of person even if your relationships continue to end

Try to negotiate points with a person with various objectives for the future

Stay in a relationship which isn't going anywhere. Maybe you're not virginal, but maintain attracting visitors to non-monogamy people. You give non-monogamy with a shot, over every time, but get upset and even injured every time. Perhaps you'd like to have children and your partner doesn't. Everything else is working, so you're still in the group and hope that they will change their minds. If you're in these kinds of situations you're preventing on yourself from finding someone who is a better fit in the in the long run.

It is difficult to begin your demands

If you are having a hard in expressing yourself, you could be unable to get all your desires met.

This could happen in:

family members ' situations

amongst friends

at work

with charming partners

in everyday communications

The scene where you stand in the line at the store eating a sandwich, when an individual carrying a full cart of food items cuts right in front of you. You're in a rush and want to return to your work however, you are unable to bring yourself to take any of the items. Then you let them continue and arrive late to the conference you can not afford to be late for.

Your very own position down

People typically set a number of higher expectations for themselves own than they do for their fellow citizens. If you don't fulfill these standards then you might be confronted with some very harsh remarks:

" I'm not able to do any thing, isn't it."

" I'm not going to do it therefore why bother?"

" Wow, I messed up. I'm not good with this."

If you are adamant about your own in front of other people or employ a strategy of self-deflection that is damaging The same thing is likely to occur: Your remarks may be believed to be factual. If you think about these criticisms, they can lead to an attitude of self-defeat and also keep you from trying again. At some point, you could give up before you even begin.

What is the cause?

According to Joseph self-sabotage occurs when you engage in certain actions that you could have adapted to in one situation, but don't have the same significance in another. In simple terms this way, they allowed you to adapt to an old situation that was stressful, such as a difficult young adult year or toxic relationship and also overcome the obstacles you encountered. They may have helped you or helped you. However, these strategies of dealing with stress can lead to problems as your circumstances change.

Here's a deeper analysis of some of the many contributing factors.

Childhood patterns are discovered during childhood.

The relationships that we form in our first relationships often replicate in relationships throughout our lives according to Joseph. "We're stuck to these relationships. They represent something to us, and also because they're difficult to leave," Joseph states.

Say you had parents who didn't give much attention on you unless you were upset.

" You realize it's not a great decision to get people to go crazy," Joseph states, "Nonetheless they're a lot of fun due to this education. Making people angry was the only way to increase interest, and you're stuck in this cycle that is attractive, appealing and also to make people angry about you." This could be evident for instance in your work environment, when you are unable to be on time. Initially, your boss is flexible and encourages you to work, however the time goes by and you are unable to show up on time and your boss is unable and eventually releases you.

Previous link's attributes

If you did not feel appreciated or heard when you asked what you wanted in your previous relationships, whether charming or otherwise it could be difficult to be a productive participant in the current relationship. If you were an unkind partner or one who did not respect your opinions as well as emotions, you might not have been able to assert yourself. You were hesitant to speak up to protect yourself from being disregarded, and other unpleasant situations. However, this is because you didn't discover any way the opportunity to fulfill your desires. Your current situation is different from your past, however it's not easy to overcome the same destructive patterns.

Be afraid of failure

If you do not want to fail in the pursuit of your dream job or in your relationship or even as a wonderful parent, you could accidentally hinder your efforts to perform good.

The desire to avoid failure may cause you to steer clear of making any attempt. If you aren't willing to try it, you will not fail. Your subconscious mind could offer you validations, but can also be a means of putting yourself down. In the image, you're part of the midst of a newer relationship that's going extremely well. Well, you believe that it's just a matter timing before you get something to complete it. "This is fantastic," you inform on your own. "It isn't going to last forever."

You don't want to face the consequences and so you start to withdraw from your partner, shutting you off emotionalally, as well as launching discussions. In normal conversations, you're enticed to create your own way of stopping, so you're not stunned when you see it happen.

A need for control

Self-sabotaging behaviors can also result the need to control the situation. If you remain at the helm, you can be confident, secure and ready to face any challenge that comes your way. Self-sabotage can give you this sense of control. The actions you're taking may be detrimental to your health, or your relationships but it will help you remain in control when you're vulnerable.

Let's consider the lazy instance. You might be putting off your research due to the fact that deep inside, you're concerned that you won't be able to write it the way you'd really like to achieve. You realize that writing it in the final minute won't improve the quality of your work but it can put you in charge of that outcome since you decided to write it on time. timing.

It can also happen in relationships. The act of opening up to someone mental is a risky thing to do. In keeping points in your mind, you maintain what appears to be the edge. However, at the end the day, you'ren't receiving the benefits of affection for structure by sharing your vulnerabilities.

Tips to beat it

Things that have helped you in the past do not help you as much when the circumstances change. They usually cause some kind of injuries. But, you continue to do them because you know that they worked for you, at least once upon the time.

A silver lining? It's possible to alter self-sabotaging patterns without much effort.

Recognize the actions

It's not always easy to review your activities in depth sufficient to recall ways to self-sabotage. "Admitting that we're self-sabotaging isn't good," Joseph claims. "Nobody is quick to make that decision. We are prone to avoid it as long as we can until we are left with the choice to accept it." If you're comfortable with the idea of analysing your behavior to discover patterns, it can help in identifying areas of the world where points appear all the time.

Are there any particular elements that are noticeable? For instance, maybe you have cut off connections and began picking fights when your friend says, "I like you." Perhaps you've the habit of putting off tasks prior to your annual assessment.

Find out what sets you apart

If you are able to identify the ways you're threatening your self be aware of when you are doing these things. What are the signs that you make you appear as you need to perform?

Perhaps the angry tone of the voice of your friend reminds you of the scolding you received in your early years. You are constantly shutting down even when the anger doesn't get out to you.

Other triggers that can put self-sabotaging behaviors into action are:

monotony

Concern

elements that work

Insecurity

Record your triggers and write them down in a journal. The practice of mindfulness or nonjudgmental acceptance of your thoughts and behaviors in the present moment may help.

When you discover an event that triggers you, come one or two powerful ways to modify the self-sabotaging behavior.

Technique for getting comfortable with failure

It's normal to worry about being rejected, a failure as well as other emotional aches. These issues are usually unpleasant to deal with and you take action to avoid these issues. It can be a problem in the event that your actions are self-sabotage. You may decide to leave bad events, but you're likely to lose out on things you'd like to have for example, good friendships, solid relationships or job opportunities.

To handle this concern be able to accept the reality of failure and discomfort. This is an extremely difficult task and it will not happen over night. Begin by trying to discover the reason you're failure, regardless of whether it's an affair that has gone south or missed an opportunity in the workplace or as an chance to gain.

The conclusion of this collaboration means that you'll finally be able to appeal to the adorable barista. Perhaps the slack on task could mean you'll have quite a bit of time to relax before you can get back to your favorite pastime.

Discuss it

If you notice certain patterns that keep popping up on your websites, try speaking with the people you're closest to about these patterns. You could try saying this to your friend: "I desire our link to work. However, I'm worried about the link failing. If I appear to detach or withdraw in the middle of the night, it's because i'm waiting to be lost. I'm working to conquer it but I don't wish to convince you that I'm not interested about it in the meantime." In the words of Joseph, simply speaking about an self-sabotaging behavior in public can stop you from bringing it up. Also, it could be a beneficial learning experience when the situation is portrayed in different waysand not on the path of self-sabotage.

Recognize what you truly want

Self-sabotage can happen when you're looking for an escape. These behaviors can indicate an aspect of your life that's not working for you.

If you're feeling unsatisfied at working because your daily work doesn't make use of any of your skills that you are skilled in You could start watching Netflix when you're exhausted.

Or , you can inform yourself that you're looking for to connect, even though you're more comfortable being single. When you get past the laid-back dating stage, you're having problems. Knowing more about your own, and identifying your goals in life could help in avoiding self-sabotage. It's not enough to know the things you want, but. You must also be aware and assist yourself to make the most of it.

The best time to search for support

It's sometimes difficult to identify and give up certain self-defeating practices, particularly the patterns you've followed for a long time, independently. If your attempts to test different activities as well as actions haven't worked or have not helped you for a while the treatment could be a good option.

It's not a shame to seek professional help.

" There's a possibility that there's something that you don't recognize," Joseph says. "In some instances it's impossible to uncover all the underlying aspects by yourself."

Treatment is particularly effective to self-sabotage since over a prolonged period it is possible to accidentally start doing something wrong during treatment. A professional can be able to detect this. In addition, help brings the issue, which you may not have been conscious of to the forefront.

The following overview of the treatment options for all budgets will help you take the first step.

The most important thing is the bottom line

Self-sabotaging behaviors are usually embedded in your life and are difficult to identify. Additionally, even the moment you recognize them the way you hold onto your own back may be difficult to come to accept. But remember that when you acknowledge these behaviors, you've taken the first step towards of changing these habits. It is not necessary to tackle it on your own. People like them in the group, and also experienced experts can offer assistance.

You might be wondering what it takes to beat that art contestant. But in contrast to saying, "Why trouble?" and also squeezing on the type, you should fill it up and complete your very best job. What you learn on your own could have similar value to getting the job done.

Chapter 7: Habits And Instincts

One of the most important factors to take into consideration to ensure that you succeed in hacking your mind the fact that some types of thinking and behavior might be more difficult to alter.

This could be due to the fact that these are behaviors that we've been trained into , and instincts that are natural as survival tools.

A. Habits

I was once smoking.

I began smoking cigarettes with the same people who taught me to take drugs. Like all drugs smoking, smoking cigarettes doesn't affect your the daily routine.

It was, in fact, an enjoyable break from the stress that was going through my head at the time.

I wasn't a big smoker at all, not even compared to other smokers I used be acquainted with. Most likely, I used to smoke about seven cigarettes per day.

Every cigarette I smoked was associated with an occasion. For instance when I woke and rinsed my mouth initial thing that I did was to smoke cigarettes. Also, I smoked after every meal. Another one after brushing my teeth after dinner before going to go to bed.

Another time I smoked a cigarette, I felt tired, stressed or uncomfortable for any reason.

As you might have thought, I have just reaffirmed my habit by smoking regularly. I correlated smoking with my sleeping/wake cycles as well as my meals. I also attributed it to my issues.

It definitely brought some relief and a pleasant nicotine buzz that was great with coffee, but , of course it was not good to me health.

It was the final thing I let go of in the end, actually.

Every time I got up and didn't smoke my day was a blur. Every time I ate, and didn't smoke, it found myself feeling like I was unable to get my food down. If I didn't smoke when I was feeling anxious or upset or upset, then I'd just feel anxious and angry.

It was a real struggle to give up. I attributed it to certain elements of my everyday routine.

Have you heard about the Pavlov experiment in which the man rang a bell before giving his pet food?

In the end, the dog equated the bell with food. It's the way I treated myself. I thought that smoking was associated and certain kinds of things.

As a dog would expect to be fed after it received the call I was hoping to have my cigarettes the moment I awoke when I was done eating and before I went to sleep.

Habits are extremely effective, and some can totally take over your life.

However, the fact is that behaviors aren't restricted to smoking cigarettes. There are other practices that could be more abstract for instance, fearing certain things referred to as phobias, or specific behaviors like nail biting.

Each habit was born out of the need to find some type of ease. Sometimes the root of the problem is fear or aversion, but the point I want to make is that the reason for habits typically arise out of the need to be comfortable.

And, since this need was fulfilled at an element through the new method You could repeat it repeatedly until you no longer is conscious of what you're doing.

The Three Habits of a Habit

There are three primary ways to establish an habit. The first is the cue. For me as a smoker my cue would be awake early in the day, having eaten something, feeling overwhelmed and sleepy.

As you could imagine I was able to take a lot of cues. Cues are the primary factor that triggers behaviour which, as is the case in this instance it was an habit.

The second part is the actual act or, as it's known officially, the routine.

Once I had my cue which is basically anything that I have mentioned previously and I leave the house, grab an e-cigarette from the pack, take my lighter and then light the cigarette.

After that, I inhale smoke, then exhale. Then, I repeat this process until I've finished one smoking.

After doing this I am rewarded The third element of a routine. The reward is the result of following the routine.

In my experience I'm awestruck by the feeling of peace.

Habits eventually develop into an automatic response. The more you repeat it in the long run, it will become easier to reinforce and build it.

The longer you've had a routine, the more difficult it becomes to break it.

However, what I'm trying to get to know about habits is that they're something you've created, therefore it's something you have the ability to break.

I'm not able to give you any guarantee that this is going to be simple however mind hacking can definitely make it simpler than standard methods.

The most popular methods to get rid of the habit is replacing it with something different.

One good example is smoking vapes. In the days when in which I attempted to stop smoking cigarettes, there weren't any vapes in the beginning.

Nowadays, however smoking cessation is a common practice,

with many people substituting cigarettes with e-cigarettes and vapes. If they're feeling the need for nicotine then they pull out their vapes and breathe in the vapor.

It's claimed to be more secure than smoking cigarettes, but only the time and study will reveal whether or not.

If the intention of a smoker but, it's to replace cigarettes with something more secure, then vapes are an ideal alternative.

The desire to smoke cigarettes is still satisfied, however, it will be with something different. The actual action of smoking a cigarette the mouth has become a routine also, and that is something the action of placing a vape into your mouth is also replacing.

In essence, the behavior remains, but changed to something that is acceptable.

If you're a vaper I hope that you don't find it offensive to say that it's not a viable solution.

It's certainly an important step in the right direction but if you're planning to keep smoking cigarettes throughout the duration of your life, then there's no difference.

I've met people who use vapes, and are planning to quit smoking cigarettes however I've yet to meet someone who has quit smoking vapes.

Most of the time, the most efficient method to get rid of an habit is to get off the habit gradually. With mind hacking methods that are effective, it's going to take some time however the final outcome, if it's done properly is the complete elimination from the habit.

Although I'm sure my method begins with changing a component of a routine with another however, it's not the sole method I employ to correct it.

Additionally, I outline steps that lead to the habit being eliminated and the best way to avoid any relapses.

B. Instinct

I was once watching an animal documentary that explained the ways animals make use of their instincts. According to the documentary instincts are natural behavior "shortcuts."

To make an argument, the group displayed the bird's flightlessness; it could have been a duck or a goose, lying on its nest, which was full of tiny white eggs.

If an egg flies out of the nest the bird's instincts tell it to leave its nest, and walk toward the egg that is missing and then, with their bill, pushes it and then rolls it back into the nest.

It's very clever, right?

However, here's the issue. Since it's instinctual There's no need for analysis.

If something bears an emblazoned look to eggs, and is not nestled The bird will do the same sequence repeatedly.

They showed this first using a tiny white ball. The bird, as expected, returned it into its nest.

Then, they put the golf ball, which , to anyone else, will clearly look different than the smooth, round ball. For the bird however, it appears to be an egg, which is why it goes through the entire process and then tucks the golf ball back into its nest.

They also used the white cube. However, the bird still goes

through the entire process and is able to place the cube in its nest.

It seems that anything about the same dimensions as an egg and that is colored white, is perceived by birds it as an egg. If the object is located outside the nest and the bird is able to see it, the natural reaction is to seek out the item and return it into its nest.

Another interesting behaviour is the behavior is that Bengal tigers.

In places where tigers are found close to human beings The people living there have learned to put on masks on the rear of their heads.

The reason is because tigers prefer to take on attackers from behind. The presence of a mask on the back of their head can make the tiger believe that the person is facing them.

In the interest of updating I had this knowledge back while I was still in the elementary school So I decided to conduct some research.

Evidently, the tigers later discovered the difference between a false front and a genuine one which is why masks aren't an effective strategy to keep away attack by tigers.

But, isn't it fascinating what happened when the tigers were kept out of the way?

Tigers are much more intelligent than birds, and they have learned to adjust to human masks. They were taught to distinguish fake faces from genuine faces, however, they took on one side that was the back.

Thus, they were able alter their cues and add some steps, which included some analysis.

Humans also possess certain traits. Psychologists and scientists consider that traits such as altruism and the fight or flight mechanism are instincts.

Fight-or-flight is an instinct that allows a person to react to danger at a level that is personal, as well as altruism, which is an instinctive action that is beneficial to the human race in general.

If you sense threats the body reacts by controlling the brood pressure and breathing as well as other body functions in order to prepare you to take action. You could choose to fight, or run and run, but in either case your body has prepared itself for whatever reaction you choose.

Sometimes our instincts can go off the rails and cause our lives to become somewhat more challenging. One such instinct-gone-haywire is having intense social anxiety or panic attacks.

It's normal to be small amount of anxious about being embarrassing or being embarrassed about things.

Some people, however, exhibit extreme anxiety or shyness more than the majority of people. They are so anxious and scared that their fight or flight emotions are activated when they think about it. thinking about it, they shouldn't be worried or scared at all.

As you've likely already figured out that it is an option to manage these ailments when the person suffering of it wants to seek treatment.

The availability of medicines can help fix the imbalances in chemical that could be the cause of the condition. The people suffering from these types of ailments can also seek the assistance of counselors to solve the issue using a mental approach rather than an physical or physiological one.

Mind hacking is like taking the approach of a therapist. The sole difference is instead of hiring someone to attempt the hacking of your mind, you perform the hacking yourself.

Personally, I am a believer that therapy is effective, at the very least I've heard what I've read about it. I've never attended an AA group, but I know friends who have been regularly in for a long time and all of them swear to the efficacy in the therapy group they receive.

Sometimes all you require is others with the same struggles and struggles as you.

Maybe you're not the type to be. Perhaps you're not comfortable about sharing your concerns with people around you. Perhaps you'd rather explore solving the issue on your own .

Mind hacking is where it is a key component. It's not a substitute for therapy performed by professionals who are trained Let me be crystal clear about this.

But, there are times when people cannot afford the same treatment that my family members could before I had my addiction issues.

My mother was a difficult single mom with two kids. She would not have afforded to send me to rehabilitation.

In all this it is my sister who I consider to be the true hero. When I made the decision to return home following an overdose of heroin, my sister was absent from school for a whole week to be there for me.

My addictions and the words I used during withdrawal would have surely affected her. There were even occasions, and I'm now admitting that I even attempted to hurt her in order in order to get me out of the house, however she stood by me with a smile.

I also learned about thinking about hacking myself because I realized how my mom and sister loved me. It was due to them that I chose to make changes.

My life could be a completely different one than the one I'm currently living in if I had a less loving family.

I wouldn't be in a position to consider getting myself back in my head in the absence of the amount my family has given for me.

I was able to hack my mind out of the need. I needed to make myself better in order to prevent causing my family members any further pain and issues.

Yes, I did not want to die, and that was what motivated me but the support of my family was what kept me up and running.

It's feasible to transform your life and make it better without help

However, I'm merely suggesting that if you are able to afford it take it.

What I'd like you to remember through your journey is that you need to keep trying and learning.

While my suggestions may not work as well for you, they work for me, you could attempt to modify some elements to make your own.

The primary reason is the fact that change may feel like a battle, and if you're doing it all your own, it can be a bit more difficult.

The goal of the next chapter will be to pinpoint your triggers and cues. Next, you must identify your daily routine. Then, identify your reward.

If you've completed the exercises in Chapter 1, you'll be able to discern your thoughts clearly and become more conscious of the state of your mind each time you fall into an habit you'd like to break.

If you're experiencing lots of negative thoughts, it's something you should focus on understanding because, just like the habits that lead to negative thoughts, they can also be constructed by the potential to trigger routines and triggers.

There is no need to perform anything right now other than to be aware of your triggers or cues the routine you follow, as well as the reward.

Then, I'll show you how to begin enforcing the discipline of these habits and thoughts.

It's the topic I'll be discussing within the coming chapter on self-control as well as discipline.

I also set a rule that if I needed to buy ingredients for unhealthy fooditems, I would have to take a walk to the grocery shop and then return.

Of course I was also blocking thoughts about food. Food thoughts were kept from my mind.

I also began counting my calories. I started by finding out the amount of calories I required each day and subtracting 1,000 calories, and after that, I mentally count the calories in every drink and food I consume.

Of course, it could not have gone as smoothly without a

significant reason and at that time, my motive was to be able to appear like a bodybuilder.

I also wanted for basketball games with buddies for the first time I also did not want to take the same medication I was selling to my doctors.

I didn't turn into bodybuilder, however I did lose a lot of weight , and then got back to a weight of two-twenty pounds after 10 months.

I hope you didn't think to lose all the weight that I gained in only a month. Trust me when I say that in the beginning stages of planning, this was the goal I set for myself.

However I realized that it wasn't healthy to shed so many pounds over such a small period of time.

Additionally, as I stated earlier it takes time for habits to change. When I made the decision to alter the way I eat, I'd had a binge eating habit for over an entire year. It wasn't feasible to believe that the habit would change, and my cravings to be squelched within such a short period of time.

I know that this is probably not what you expected to learn about. You might have expected my ability to figure it out in just a few hours and then losing the weight in one months time, however it isn't that easy or at all when you're trying to be a good person.

The truth is, discipline and self-control isn't something that you master in a day. However, you should begin to be strict with yourself the moment you make the decision to do so. You'll also be extremely effective in a couple of days.

The problem is that the enthusiasm and desire to keep your desires in check will fade after a couple of days. In the initial couple of days you'll naturally extremely motivated and excited and it will appear quite easy.

However, as the hours pass your motivation and enthusiasm are going to fade until they're gone. And you may return to the same routine you've been doing after the novelty is over.

What you need is a gradual increase. It is not a good idea to initiate an enormous change in the nick of time and exhaust all the motivation and enthusiasm.

Making it gradual with consistency is the true factor in achieving making a change. It's not overwhelming motivation or determination, but a steady small dose of it and commitment to the desired goal.

Start small, build up gradually and slowly increase the amount.

Here's the assignment for this chapter.

I'm guessing that by now, you have a good idea of how to meditate and clear your mind and know how to identify your patterns by triggers, your routine and what you can expect from your reward.

I would like you to begin contemplating and discover the main motivation behind this thing that you'd like to change.

I would like you to sit down and remind yourself that you must make a change. I'd like you to develop a framework or plan you can make this change happen within a reasonable timeframe.

I want you to put your efforts towards identifying the factors that trigger the behavior you'd like to alter, and then reduce the exposure you have to them.

I would also like that you make it more difficult or more complex to follow the routine you have created by adding additional steps to the routine, which will make it seem harder.

Of course, I'd like you to take action on what you've come up with. It's not enough to leave it all in your mind. Unarticulated thoughts are only thoughts. You must take action on them to turn them into reality.

121

In the next section, I'll inform you what many refer to as the state of "flow," where many successful people draw their most innovative concepts to.

The next section we'll discuss more about focus. This will aid you to achieve the state of hyperfocus.

Chapter 8: Self-Sabotage
Health And The Body

It is not really a matter of that you're unwell or in a position to not manifest joy and prosperity in your life , because your body is unable to cooperate as you'd like it to. It is likely that there's an unconscious program that is hidden behind that.

It is possible for a disease to arise from many unfavorable beliefs. The structure and patterns of our thoughts and the way our brain is taught to function, is a powerful influence on the body and its functions.

There are a variety of trained and learned patterns can be found here. This means that we have learned and copied family patterns about how certain issues were resolved through illness. We keep doing this since we do not have other methods of dealing with and dealing with issues.

The disease always comes with two outcomes:

There is a way to avoid something.

You are able to get something you could not otherwise.

Also, we are talking about secondary profits, also known as secondary profits. This means that even the issue that's bothering you could also bring about something positive to your advantage. Perhaps you're not conscious of it.

Let's find out these secrets step-by-step.

It is not a pleasure to be sick, we're all on this. However, it is true that disease can be a source of pain and can be used as a method to gain or reach something that cannot be achieved or gained in any other way. It is unlikely that anyone does it on purpose or even aware of it.

It can give us the attention, love or even sympathy that we might never get elsewhere. It also offers relief and relaxation when we are unable to accomplish it in other manner. It could even make others to do something that they would not do. It can be an instrument of authority and power, that you could never enjoy without it.

However, it could also free us from things. There are some things we can't do when we are sick, which can be a valid reason to be excused. It is possible for illness to keep someone or something from us. This means that we can quickly escape from situations without fear of losing face or causing conflict.

Sometimes, we fall ill for the family or even a specific individual. This can be a means to be in touch with someone who is sick, or who may have died recently. From a holistic point of the horizon, health issues may require a person to take care of something so that it doesn't collapse and fall apart. Guilt is a burden carried by the majority of us. In a way, this is normal and we ought to be able to manage it. However, when it becomes grave or we feel that we must take on the guilt of of our ancestors, illness is the only option to avenge ourselves or to be a victim to ourselves.

If you do not permit or encourage happiness and pleasure to be a part of your life, then disease can be a fantastic way to deny it. Maybe your parents happen to be sick or miserable and you're not permitted to be happier or more healthy that they did? Do you know of a beloved human being who die prematurely and now you're connected with that person through using a similar illness?

In this moment, I have to talk about something of immense significance in this particular situation. If you are aware of it, it can bring about a significant changes to you or someone within your immediate vicinity.

People subconsciously carry some sort of death wish in themselves. They seek out the way to die and consequently become ill or develop an addiction. The cause for wishes to die usually lies in the fact that a parent has died too young, so the child wants to remain close to the parent. It is also possible to apply to any other relative within the system. It is crucial to be aware of this. The misguided relationship needs to be guided towards healthier ways to allow life to evolve and be attainable again. The bond to and affection towards someone can be felt but without a self-defeating fashion.

If these tendencies are present and are present, they can be cured or addressed by the program and some of the rituals to resolve them. If you're struggling with depression or addiction that is severe I recommend asking for advice from an experienced therapist for a time to take a more detailed review of your patterns of behavior. It's o.k. asking for help. There is no need to tackle every problem by yourself. The pain you feel is a sign or a sign that something within you is holding you from moving forward and preventing your way to real-life living.

Perhaps it was not an option to deal with or deal with a emotional or personal grief you went through. You may not have had the opportunity to end your relationship with the person you love. Assistance from a professional could help you navigate how to get back into your life, and help you regain the strength to live the life you want to. This program can be a huge assistance in this direction however, sometimes it's essential to have a skilled professional at your side to guide you to a state of renewal and regenerative. Don't be afraid to take risks!

The general rule is that any type or kind of illness can be used to cope with the rigors of life. For many families, the answer to major challenges is illness. However, instead seeking a cure,, it just creates more issues.

A lot of us haven't been taught how to handle issues, desires, or concerns in a positive and healthy manner. In the next chapter of this book you will discover and master the various ways that you can, in the future take on situations in a different manner.

In the section on program in this book, you'll find methods to identify the subconscious beliefs that are the source of your illness. At this point, you will be able to determine the goal you're trying get through the disease and what it really means by asking yourself some smart questions.

* What isn't possible because of my condition?

* What can be accomplished through it? What is not possible or be possible without it?

* What would happen in the event that I were healthy? What do I need to do and what would I be able to do?

What would I be lacking if I was healthy?

* Who would be against me if I was healthy?

* What are my chances of self-punishment? Do I feel guilt-filled about some thing?

Don't be concerned if you are unable to locate the answers you need right now. You'll find them in the exercises later. If you have felt any guilt, you'll be able to change them by undergoing the rituals in the future.

If you are feeling overweight or underweight, it is because there is some beliefs that prevent your body from operating free of limitations. Due to this, an instinctual feeling of being overwhelmed or a healthy lifestyle have little chance of kicking in. Each diet is destined to fail if there's an implicit belief that tells you that you're overweight, which makes you want to consume more food. If you are feeling your weight as a way to protect yourself, then you automatically create this feeling. If you experience an empty feeling inside and have adopted this belief and this void will be filled by food. No diet is going to help to stop the urge to follow. If your mind's subconscious believes that you're only "somebody" for as long as you've got an enormous, massive body, or feel that you're gaining weight in this manner and all you have to do is eat in order to achieve the objectives.

Together we'll uncover your own personal reasons for being overweight and the reasons you're not able to fight it.

Martin Martin, who has been battling to lose weight for nearly

15 years has the following
beliefs:

* , "I'm not happy with how my
body looks, something isn't
performing well."

* "As long as my body is obese
I'll be able to do many things."

*,, I need to make a payment
between my parents. They are
each tearing me apart. I'll need a
lot more weight to cope with
this."

*,I'm insufficient."

* "I am scared of being close."

Just by revealing these
obstacles and becoming fully
conscious of them , as well as
having a conversations about
what truly matters in our lives,

we were able to achieve instant success, without the necessity for any additional transformation work. The man lost 55 pounds in an entire year.

The recognition of the unconscious beliefs as well as the awareness of what is important and essential in his life helped him achieve. He's worked with many trainers and programs but with no success. He achieved his goal by working with a only trainer, and very quickly.

It was possible due to this time , he felt the body in a gentle and loving way . He was able to realize that as a mature adult and a man of his own, he's not with his parents anymore, and is completely free. The moment he realized this, he was now ready to confront the issues that he'd been trying to avoid throughout through his entire life e.g. the real and genuine closeness with an attractive female partner. He began to focus on it on a regular basis. He is now aware the importance of self-worth as a right and that he is sufficient just the way the way he is.

It's o.k. when everything is simple. It's o.k. when you're feeling relaxed. You deserve the complete bliss and happiness you can find without any major challenges.

Let's put this knowledge into action - one step at a time towards peace and prosperity. Let me help you and guide you to becoming the true "you" who is completely at ease with all your choices.

Chapter 9: Procrastination

A real issue of our time Procrastination is the root cause for the majority of our everyday mistakes, both small and large. We often be funny and laugh about this, but it's a actual issue. The act of putting off work, particularly in schools or at work isn't just selfish and self-indulgent, it's in fact, it can be dangers. Your boss will not be pleased to see you wasting time in idleness during office hours instead of working hard. In fact, it might even get you kicked out.

Of course this is something that you've already heard about; it's something we all do it. Why do you continue doing it? Why do we all? Perhaps it's due to lazyness, part insufficient awareness, part confidence in your capabilities, and part the time frame you're required to complete an assignment completed. "I don't want to complete this task today, I'll begin later. I have a few hours to go." Do you recognize the words?

Procrastination can consume huge amounts of your time, and whether you are aware of that or not, the habit to delay the tasks you must do can be causing harm to yourself. You are just sabotaging yourself in the process of finding excuses or getting behind when it comes to finishing the task. If you suffer the consequences, who's the sole one to blame? Yourself!

It's extremely tempting to put off completing your task especially when you dislike the job, chore or task you have to complete

However, you must be thinking about whether it's worthwhile or not. It's not like if you leave it unfinished it, it will go away. It's still going to be necessary to address it in the near future. Now that you're behind You're probably being squeezed by time, and you could be overwhelmed or in a in a panic, trying to complete.

It's true that this has a significant impact on the overall effectiveness of your work. Although it may appear that you're more inventive and efficient when you're doing all the work in a hurry in the midst of a ever-present deadline, but it's far from the truth. You're actually trying to complete everything and don't pay enough attention to the task at hand. You don't commit the needed time, you don't edit it as thoroughly as you ought to and the final result isn't as good. Don't tell yourself you've done an excellent job just because you did it a few times It is always evident the effort you put into something, and also when you made up something in the last minute to meet your deadline.

Do not become the person - you've seen what I'm talking to you about. If you put off work you are viewed as the lazy one who doesn't focus on their work in a timely manner. This is bound cause problems and impact your work performance in many ways. Be aware that putting off work is to undermine yourself or your work as well as your image.

The Solution

The solution to the procrastination issues you have may be easy; you simply need to be motivated to stop this circumstance that's not helping you in any way. There are some basic, easy things you can try to get rid of the temptation to delay and boost your productivity.

Eliminate distractions

This is the simplest and most likely method to reduce procrastination, or end it completely. This is logical, doesn't it? If there's nothing to distract you and pull you towards the darker side of life, you'll be able to stay focused and complete your task quickly and punctually. It sounds simple enough in principle however it's a lot more challenging in actual practice.

This could mean that you'll have to say goodbye to your blatant internet usage. The internet is the most adolescent time-waster of all time and it's very easy to be lost in a puddle of cat videos or funny Reddit posts. Be sure to not use the internet for personal use when you're working or when you're at home and trying to finish your studies, complete an assignment , or finish whatever task you're currently working on.

If you have to do something drastic to block your preferred websites, you can block them as well as push notification notifications for social networks on your smartphone - at a minimum, temporarily. You'll get lots more done in less time if you're not constantly interrupted for two or more minutes with an enthusiastic scream that announces that someone had commented on your most recent Facebook post. It's better to leave that for the future.

Family, friends and pets are also considered "distractions" that means you must inform your family members, friends and roommates that they can't distract you when you're working on something crucial. It could be beneficial to take a break and retreat to a place that you're free of distractions like conversations, meowing, music or noises from the television. If it's not urgent the roommate is able to wait until later, as will your preferred show. You can also enjoy some quality time with your cat. Sorry, Fluffy.

Set limits

You can get assistance from outside sources to help you deal in overcoming your procrastination issue however, it's your responsibility to motivate your own self to put off things and begin becoming effective and productive. A great way to help towards that end is setting yourself specific limitations. Limits on time, that's what.

It's a simple and easy task real-worldly assess the time it would be to complete a task , and then establish an time frame. You must complete your work within the specified timeframe regardless of the task. It doesn't need to be a situation that you can replicate but you could do some tests to make sure you are familiar with working within a specific time frame. This won't just "train" the mind to not procrastinate and putting off work, but also help you become organized and efficient, and also to be effective when it comes to deadlines. I can't stress enough how valuable this knowledge can be later in life even if you're not currently faced by a working environment in which you'll need it.

Since every effective training program includes an element of "treat" to reward an excellent job It's an excellent idea to give yourself something after you've completed the task with little or no interruption and with no wasted time. This way, you'll feel more motivated and eager to complete with the knowledge that something you love is waiting for when you reach the conclusion. Positive reinforcement can be very effective but you must try it and, most importantly be motivated to finally remove yourself from the

self-sabotaging habit of putting
off work.

Chapter 10: The Foods That Boost Mind Control

It's no surprise that brain activity
is influenced by the food we eat,
and responds to the nutrients it
receives. All people should
consume food which are healthy
for the whole body, including the
brain. Researchers have
discovered an uncanny link
between food sources and the
control of people's willpower. It's
easy for someone to alter their
thinking capacity and ability to
focus by making some changes
to their food habits. This doesn't
require consulting any
nutritionist and all one has to do

is to incorporate certain "brain food items" in their diet.

In this section we examine all the top foods effective in helping people be more self-controlled and boost their willpower. These are foods which are readily available and don't require you to put an effort for them.

Eggs

Eggs are fantastic brain foods. Not only can they increase self-control but can also boost your memory and brain's overall capacity. They're loaded with proteins needed by the brain in order to stay fit and functioning optimally. They also help to prevent cortisol's excessive release which could hinder the brain's functioning. A serving of two eggs daily is sufficient and give you the chance to receive the protein intake you need. It is possible to incorporate eggs into your daily diet by having them in a scrambled form for breakfast, or having eggs boiled as snacks.

Fish

Fish oils are crucial to brain development. They are packed with omega 3 fatty acids , which are necessary to ensure proper brain development. Additionally, they include DHA as an acid essential in the development and control of brain. Anyone who eats fish oils on a regular basis will be able to maintain cardiovascular health. Since the brain and the heart are closely linked and interconnected, they will have a more effective control of the body and mind. Consuming cod or salmon since they are rich in natural oils. If you're a vegetarian, you can consume flax seeds since they have a high amount of omega 3.

Chocolate

Dark chocolate is thought to be a good brain food that allows you to exercise more self-control. It is because it can reduce cravings as well as improve cognitive function due to its flavonols that help reduce the damage caused by oxidation. Together, these factors can help you steer away from temptations, and will give you an excellent probability of not getting distracted by a few things. Dark chocolate is a treat to eat as a whole, and you can eat two small pieces a day. It is also possible to incorporate it into your meals and cook both savory and sweet ones, as this type of chocolate isn't very sweet.

Fresh greens

Fresh green sprouts as well as leafy green vegetables and green fruits are excellent for your brain. They will assist your mind to be clear and be able to eliminate all poisons out of your brain. They will improve the function of your liver, which allows the ammonia to be transformed into urea and removed from your body before it has the chance to get into the brain. This will improve the function of your brain and allow you to think more clearly. You can use them in any way you prefer and include sprouts in your salads. You can also use the green fruits in fruit salads and so on.

Oranges

Oranges are a great source of vitamin C, which is beneficial for your entire body. They can help eliminate toxic substances from your body. In addition, your brain will be healthy and clear throughout the day. The possibility of fatigue developing is avoided by eating foods that contain vitamin C. It is possible to eat an whole orange every day on a regular basis and then juice it to drink at ease. It is also possible to consume grapefruits, lemons as well as other fruits of the citrus since they all aid in limiting the damage that oxidative causes to your brain. It will also prevent free radicals from forming that will keep your brain healthy for a long time.

Seeds

Seeds are a wealth of nutrients that are vital to the brain. They are believed to be rich in nutrients that let the person remain alert throughout the day, and to fight off distracting thoughts with vigor. The oils release from these seeds feed the brain and help people to concentrate. It is possible to eat the roasted peanuts or almonds at times and they make the ideal snack options. You can also include sunflower and pumpkin seeds because they are also beneficial in improving brain functioning. Roast and grind them, then sprinkle over curries and salads.

Oats

Oats are a great brain food. They are believed to be rich in antioxidants and aid in reducing cholesterol and reducing it to a minimum. Cholesterol is known to impair the brain's function and can also lead to heart issues. In order to reduce this chemical, it's possible to live a better life. Oats can be made into breakfast or can be cooked and served alongside salads. While it is typically served with fresh fruit however, you can add in some spices to create an savory meal from it. You can serve it with fresh vegetables.

Whole grains

Whole grains are the best option for your body. They can provide the nutrition of your mind and give you an improved body. Whole grains consist of barley, whole wheat and oats. and can keep you fit and active throughout the day. Avoid white rice and white flour as they supply your body with excessive carbohydrates that can slow the body and mind. Additionally, they pose the risk of cortisol release which can further limit the brain's capacity. Consider incorporating whole wheat items into your diet and opt for wheat bread instead of bread that is regular.

Broccoli

Broccoli as you are aware is considered to be one of the most vital vegetables that you can consume. It is a rich source of nutrients that are vital to the body as well as the mind. It helps enhance brain function and lessen the effects of oxidative damage. It is possible to steam or boil broccoli and then add it to salads or curries. It is possible to spice it up however you want, but be slow with salt because it could cause vital nutrients to disappear. If you're not able to consume it in its entirety and want to make smoothies with it with honey and coconut milk that is fresh to reduce the taste.

Tomatoes

The tomatoes are excellent for brain health. They are rich in lycopene, which is an anti-oxidant and can help reduce the damages caused by free radicals. They are also beneficial for overall health and aid in improving the immune system. They can be added in salads, and it's recommended to eat the tomatoes raw since cooking them can result in the loss of vital nutrients. If you must cook them, you can cook them in hot water for few seconds prior to placing them in cool water since it will aid the nutrients remain locked into the tomato and it won't taste like raw.

Olive oil

Olive oil is thought to be the best option for your body. It also can have a significant effect on your brain. It is beneficial to your brain because it is very light and doesn't overwhelm your cells with gritty odor. It is not overweight after eating meals cooked in the oil. You can add it to your salads, or drizzle it on your soups. Olives can also be included into your diet since they are a good source of essential oils. They can be poached and included in salads. You can eat olives in brined form.

Things to be aware of

It's evident that there are both positive things that can benefit your brain as well as bad ones. The negative effects of these substances can weaken the brain's function and lead to loss of control of yourself. This can significantly decrease the power of your mind and increase productivity and make your mind more unstable. It is crucial to avoid these actions. A few of them are described under.

Alcohol

Consuming a lot of alcohol can cause impairment to the brain's functioning. You've probably noticed that you lose control over your mind or thoughts when drunk, and you will be doing or saying things you will not even remember after you're clean. Gradually, your mind is going to degrade and you'll not be able to comprehend it. In the end, you'll start losing control of your thoughts and be unable manage your thoughts or thoughts. Limit yourself to 1 drink each week and select things that are light. If you're having difficulty in overcoming your drinking habits think about consulting with therapy.

Junk food

Junk food is loaded with unneeded chemicals that could cause your brain to become confused. The majority of people view junk food as just a threat to their body, but it also damages their brains too. The person who eats it will begin to lose their mental capacity and may cause them to lose their ability to think to a great degree. It can cause them to lose control over their thoughts and, consequently, it's essential to stay free of junk food as much as is possible. Beware of eating at fast food outlets and grabbing a snack at the movies. It is possible to bring your lunch to work because the cafeteria could serve unhealthy food items.

Foods processed for processing

Foods that are processed, such as chips cakes, biscuits, cakes and sodas are packed with toxic chemicals. They are often added as preservatives and may cause your brain to suffer significant damage. A lot of people are unaware when they buy a box of "healthy biscuits" and expose our bodies and minds to harmful harmful chemicals found in junk food. Avoid all processed foods and make your own snacks and take them with you wherever you go. This includes picnics, outings at the office, and theatres.

Smoking

Smoking can cause the brain cells to die. It will be difficult to think clearly and , with time, you may develop degenerative disorders. Therefore, it is essential to quit smoking as quickly as you can. You may want to go to a rehab facility if you're finding it difficult to stop smoking. It's likely that you won't be able to quit at once and should take it in your own time. Also, you must avoid any kind of organization that tries to force you to smoke , and then go to the old habits.

Drugs for recreation

Drugs can cause the same effects on your mind as cigarettes do. In reality, they could be more potent in making you lose control of your thoughts which is why it's imperative to quit using drugs as soon as possible. If you've been using for a long time it is likely that your brain is in need of every assistance it can get. Therefore it is essential to get involved in a rehabilitation program and attempt to at reducing some of the harm. Beware of those who force you to use substances and stay as far away from it as you can.

These are the different food and lifestyle-related choices you must take to boost your self-control, increase your willpower and, ultimately, increase your performance.

Chapter 11: Transitioning Into A New Paradigm

Making Personal Power

I would like be sure to let you know that the book packed full of useful information that will help you get moving forward in your journey to change your life, but what I share will not be of any use if you aren't taking action. In the preface to this book we'll be participating in things that can help in changing your life. The reason for the activities are to enthuse you. The best method to engage yourself in any task is to get you to note it down. Therefore, in your process of creating an entirely new way of thinking, I hope you're becoming aware the need to establish new routines. If you're only reading but not performing the exercises, you will not fully be able to comprehend the changes that are needed.

I've read numerous books that advise that you should do something and provide you with all this amazing information, but they don't provide you with the steps to start and keep the modifications. Be assured that I've been there and am saying that the most important elements that can bring you outcomes in life are your belief system and the speed at which you implement of huge action. This being said, I strongly suggest that you try any and all exercises that we discuss throughout this publication. Make sure you get the most value for your money because precisely that's what I'm going give you.

Exercise 3:

New paradigms are being created.

After we've rid ourselves of the old beliefs that were limiting us and have lost influence over our thinking and actions, we must change them into strong, emotional belief systems that can help us achieve our goals and happiness. To do this, I recommend that you take an A4-sized piece of paper and split the paper into three sections.

1. Life

2. You

3. Money

If you're writing down these beliefs, I'd like you to put yourself in a state of complete certainty. Think about the life you wish to lead. Are you succeeding? Are you able to follow through and consistently achieve your objectives? Are you wealthy in health? Are you awash in money? Do you run your own business, or do you frequent vacation? Consider what you'd like to achieve. Know one thing that is always the case.

Napoleon Hill said it best. "Whatever you can think of, the brain will imagine. The mind can accomplish."

It is always the same throughout your life. In the past, people believed that human beings could fly, however two brothers were able to fly. They believed in the notion so much that the universe helped them to implement this idea and make it an actuality. Nowadays, people can fly anywhere in the world they want. In the past, in order to speak to someone, you had to write an email or take the trip to visit them in person. There was a time in which a man believed it was possible to create an instrument that let people to talk to anyone they desired, no matter the location you resided in. The man in question is Steveander Graham Bell and he revolutionized how we communicate in the present. The ability to think of an idea, along with the determination to realize it will always produce the results you desire.

Once you've envisioned all you'd like to achieve, take a note of it down. Be precise and specific about what you'd like to achieve. What values do you wish to establish that will form the foundation of your life from this point forward? Consider it for a moment when you're required to.

It's crucial that we transform our mentality into an attitude that empowers us and aligns with what we desire. There's a phrase from an outstanding speaker/motivator T. Harv Eker. "Be. Do. Be." In the moment you're the first to begin making changes to your life, everybody wants to know something that can bring immediate outcomes to their daily lives. They want to achieve that quick success, or so they say. So I'm here to blow up every bubble and the rest will follow. .... It's not going to happen until you've made yourself into the person you'd like to be. If you're determined to be successful, then be a success! Make your own beliefs stronger by accomplishing tasks that propel you towards your objectives. Are you looking to become millionaire? LEARN how to manage the money you already have! Everybody wants millions and million of dollars, yet I have never heard anyone ask for the wisdom and knowledge required to manage the money.

The key to having is becoming

The the billionaire Donald Trump lost billions of dollars, what allowed him to earn his money back 3, 4 and 5 times? It wasn't his wealth... It was the person he was! If you can truly realize that being the person you desire to be can allow you to enjoy the qualities that these people possess, you'll begin to realize why BEING vital. Bob Proctor put it best. If a tree is producing poor-quality fruit or any other fruits you don't enjoy You don't cut off the fruit and wait to see different fruits. Pay attention to the seeds. If the seed is not right, the fruit will not be right. What you are is the seed and what you produce in the end is your fruit. Whatever number of times the fruit has been removed or picked; you will always be able to grow more thanks to the genetics, or the makeup of your seeds.

I would like you to succeed. This isn't about becoming rich fast to resolve all your issues or getting angry at the creator for the existence you've been given. NO. God created you, so you are able to create as well. He's provided you with all the tools needed to live your ideal life. What I'm trying to teach you is how you can better utilize the tools already in your life. You're already creators; it's just a matter of learning how to utilize your tools to a greater extent that will help you create the life that you desire and help to ensure your happiness.

Start by defining what you would like to be in the present. You'll then start to take action and complete the things you need to do and it will become natural to you. Being will lead you to do and it will lead to you having. You will attract the people, things and conditions that are necessary to build the life you envision for yourself. Then, go back to the practice.

At this point, you should already have an outline of the beliefs within each area that help you achieve your goals in the area in which you live. These beliefs

should give you
confidence! They must be beliefs
you must have in order to
achieve success throughout your
daily life. These beliefs include:

I'm abundant, I have a healthy
body, am thankful I'm the best I
am, I am happy I'm confident, I
know there's always a chance for
me, etc.

We are proving our New Beliefs

Did I mention that we always find
ways to confirm our beliefs? The
same should be the case with
the new beliefs we are
forming. We must affirm the
beliefs we have by every means
possible to reach our goals that
we have established for
ourselves. This will lead to the
results we would like to be able
to see on our behalf, in the lives
of our own and our finances,
relationships, etc.

Imagine the person you would like to be at least two times every day. In the morning, after you rise and another time at night when you are going to bed. These are the two periods that you feel the most relaxed and are also in a dream-like state. I prefer to refer to this as the state of infinite possibility. This is because, when we think, if we're flying through our dreams, then we're flying. Every thing that happens in our dreams is as real as it can be to us. But there's a catch to our fantasies. They are only true because of our belief that that it's true. It is possible to get up from the dream, and write new stories. I've done it several times. I've had dreams where I woke up from the dream and began to make various scenarios. Then you realize that, as I said that your mind is unable to discern the difference between a dream and the real world. This is why children weep on the bedding often, because they think they're actually going to the bathroom.

Use this advantage to your advantage!

Imagine who you would like to be by picturing yourself as that person. Imagine the qualities you wish to exhibit. Outgoing, charismatic, enthusiastic, a great deal maker, confident, etc. Imagine where you would like to be and who you wish to be for five to ten minutes each day at the beginning of the day and in the evening. Develop a habit of doing this by sticking to the new routine for the duration of 31 days. I'll explain more about why it's important to be a period of 31 days in the section on guidance in the book.

Remember my previous post about Wherever Focus goes , energy flows? This is precisely what's happening by using the visualizations. When you imagine your traits such as your brand new vehicle, your money and business, that vacation you'd like to take or anything else send out the vibrations that draw those items into your life. A key element of those visualizations are feelings. Many people believe that it's the things they desire, and that's the reason they do everything to achieve them. However, it's not just the tangible things, but rather the sensation that these things give. Take a moment to think about it. If you're looking to succeed, it's because you're secure, confident, wanted and strong. If you're seeking a lot of money is because you are confident, abundant, and like the kind of person who can provide, and even powerful. The great thing about this lies in the fact that you do not have to use materials to experience the feelings you would like to feel. You can make the feeling by using the material you've got or by simply creating a picture of everything happening right now. Make the experience and it creates powerful vibrations that bring those feelings to your life. Your inner self will forever make your external world. Make those feelings real and live within them.

It's the Tennis Game:

Problems to overcome when creating a better Life

I don't believe the book would do justice to those who read the book if it did not tackle issues related to the "tennis tennis match." The first time I started to shift to a new way of thinking and make the life I wanted for myself, I felt that everything was against me. I would envision my ideals, linger in that feeling and write down my goals each day, and then take huge actions. Everything was going that I was supposed to do to change my life, but everything I was experiencing in my life were circumstances which were in line with my old beliefs. Even though everyone talks about changing your life, they don't discuss the specifics of what happens in the process.

A tennis match is one that takes place in between the new manifestations you have created as well as your old manifestations. Have you heard of that you reap what you plant? This is the case both for good as well as bad things. It's not just about reaping the good results you sow. In the same way that you plant seeds that yield positive, you could also sow wrong and reap negative. What I'm trying to get you to realize is that the manifestations of your past reality could be manifesting in your life despite the brand new life you've created for yourself. I'd like to provide an opportunity to be aware of the possibility that this could occur to you, so that you are prepared. I've had it happen to me, and it's frustrating when you're trying to change your life to the best and then some old BS is revealed as a result of a belief system that you don't want to support.

I'm here to advise that you should use all obstacles as an opportunity. Learn to look beyond your current reality. The negative circumstances that come up in your life aren't meant to test you. certain are, but the majority occur because you made them. They have to develop in the end. It is essential to learn the ability to identify these forms as old inventions. It is possible to use this challenge to help strengthen yourself. You will realize that your actions, thoughts, and assumptions were in line with the old mindset you used to. Instead of being angry about the circumstances that arise then take a few moments to smile. You might look crazy, I'm not sure is happening, but you will realize that you're truly an artist.

You can say to you, "I manifested this into my life. I am the creator of what's possible within my own life." Utilize that as motivation to prove you're able to create. Learn to react to your surroundings instead of simply reacting. The difference between reacting and reacting is clear. If your reaction is to specific circumstance or another person, you allow your emotions to take over your actions. This is the reason people make statements that they did not have intended to. They are acting out of the emotions the circumstances create. Also they're controlled by external forces. When someone chooses to respond to an event, they're acting in spite of their emotions. This isn't to say you should treat all feelings as harmful in any way, but absolutely not. It is important to have emotions to motivate us to act! There's a distinct difference between using emotion to motivation to do something positive, and making the decision to let the negative emotions to dictate our actions.

The point I'm trying to say is that you should react to situations by understanding the issue. Did you invent that? Does it align with your brand new model? If not, you should ask yourself a few more questions before you make your decision.

Now I'm not the same...

What can I do to handle the situation in a way that is in line with my current self?

Do I react or respond?

It is true that in some conflict or in a stressful situation , the first thought that pops into your mind isn't the most positive thought. I can understand this. I'm not demanding you to be flawless. It's impossible. You'll fall several times, you already know? But, what is most crucial is to start to realize that you are not alone. Don't blame yourself if you do slip up. You can just make sure you catch yourself and get in the right direction. In time, you'll begin to recognize yourself, which is an amazing thing! This means you're recognizing the situation and are learning to be more aware to ensure that the next time you'll respond in a different manner.

Conclusion

There is a myriad of ways people can harm themselves. Whatever "technique" they choose to employ, whether it's alcohol abuse and self-criticism or suppression "workaholism" or any other. It's safe claim that all kinds of self-sabotage are consciously or at the very least, not easily available. The first and foremost step is to realize the existence of self-sabotage and then, to discover its specific nature. If one can discover the precise nature and method of self-sabotage, it's a lot easier to tackle this issue. In this post we've discussed a few techniques for meditation that can be utilized to improve awareness of self and mindfulness.

When one is free of self-sabotage, there's a lot of room to improve oneself, which will be a subject we'll cover in future articles. In the meantime, suffice it to say that the best strategy to avoid recurrences of self-sabotage is by focusing on specific goals.

If, after reading this article, you've spotted certain self-defeating techniques that you employ in your daily life Don't be depressed. There's always a way solve your issues and recognizing them will be the initial step to the most important goal of your life Self-actualization.

www.ingramcontent.com/pod-product-compliance
Lightning Source LLC
Chambersburg PA
CBHW060331030426
42336CB00011B/1294